HAVING A SUCCESSFUL LIFE
NO PERMISSION NEEDED

FORNEY SHELL

HAVING A SUCCESSFUL LIFE

Shell, Forney. *Having a Successful Life: No Permission Needed*

Copyright © 2022 by Forney Shell

All rights reserved.

No part of this book may be reproduced in any form or by any electronic or mechanical means, including information storage and retrieval systems, without written permission from the author, except for the use of brief quotations in a book review.

ISBNs: 978-1-7341470-2-5 (paperback) 978-1-7341470-3-2 (ebook)

Library of Congress Catalog Number: 2022911781

Cover art by Crystal Cregge | Liona Design Company

Published by KWE Publishing https://kwepub.com

Forney Shell. Having a Successful Life: No Permission Needed

CONTENTS

Preface ix
Introduction xi

1. The Meeting — 1
2. Attitude — 3
3. Society's Attitude About Success — 5
4. You and Society's Attitudes — 9
5. Education — 13
6. Self Attitude — 17
7. Attitude About Work — 23
8. Attitude About Fear — 25
9. Attitude About Failure — 27
10. Words Have Power — 29
11. Options — 33
12. Goal Setting — 35
13. Commitment — 39
14. Making And Following Plans — 41
    Epilogue — 45
    Test—Do I Deserve Success? — 51
    My Red Book Additions — 53
    Excerpts From Fred's Little Red Book — 57
    Myths About Success — 59
    Thoughts On Success — 61
    Numbers — 63
    Definitions — 65

My Thanks — 67
About the Author — 69

DEDICATION

*To my mother, my father, my Aunt Jimmy,
and all those who helped me develop self-confidence
when it could easily have gone the other way.*

PREFACE

It is natural that you would ask, what makes me qualified to write a book on becoming successful? A fair question, and one I will try to answer. The short answer is because I have been successful. You deserve a better answer than that, and I offer the following. When I was born, my dad was nineteen and my mother had just turned sixteen. Dad finished high school but my mom did not. I have two younger brothers and a younger sister. We lived in a 1000 square foot house. We never had much money, but we were a happy and close-knit family.

At an early age, I decided that I would not be poor when I grew up. I realized people would pay for knowledge they need, so I started on the trail of education. After high school I went to college and earned an associate degree in Metallurgy. This made me the first in my family to earn a college degree. Since then, I have earned a bachelor's degree in Business Management and a master's degree in Human Resource Management. For a short time, I served on the advisory board of *Human Resource Magazine*. I started my career as a trainee draftsman and retired from Boeing Aircraft as a Senior Research Design Engineer. During that career, I worked on the Minuteman missile, the Trident submarine, and contributed major designs to the Space shuttle and Moon lander projects. I hold two U.S. patents, one also applicable in England, France, and Germany. I was a member of the American Society of Optical Engineers, and am still a member of the American Society of Mechanical Engineers (ASME). I belong to the ASME committee that writes U.S. standards for engineering documentation. As part of that work, I co-authored the U.S. standards of symbology used on engineering drawings. I taught a class on dimensioning and tolerancing of mechanical parts to the American Society of Precision Engineers. I have lectured at the University of Northern Arizona, the American Society of Optical Engineers, and the Association for Electronic Manufacturing. After retiring from the aerospace industry, I moved from California to Charlottesville, Virginia, bought an acre of wooded land, and had my home built. Once settled, I took a job as a travel agent for a local agency. As an offshoot of that, I served as a professor at a local college teaching travel as a career. After fifteen years as a travel agent, at the age of eighty-two, I opened my own agency known as Pan Piper Travel. Most of the money from that venture pays for my own travel. So far, I have visited sixty-five world cities, twenty-nine countries, and taken thirty-two cruises. Many things give me pride, but nothing more than my two sons and their families. They are everything a father could ask for. They are honest caring people and each is successful in his own life endeavors.

Because of all of this I feel qualified to write about success, but that decision will ultimately be yours to make.

INTRODUCTION

It seems like we spend a great deal of our lives seeking permission: permission from our parents, our teachers, our government, and the mangers at our work. The wonderful thing about success is that it requires only your approval. Once you realize you already possess all you need to be successful, you are on your way, and you did not need to check with anyone to start the journey.

But what about the secret to wealth? People often say they wish they knew how to become wealthy. This is the weakest excuse for being less than you can be and is annoying because **there is no secret**. How could there be a secret? How to achieve wealth is one of the most talked about, written about, and widely debated of all subjects. There are hundreds of books, videos, audio tapes about it, and some well-known people make a genuinely nice income lecturing about it. If you think how to become wealthy is a secret, you are not looking in the right place, or perhaps, you are not looking at all.

There is so much information on acquiring wealth. I have chosen not to focus specifically on it. Rather, I will focus on success in general. This book speaks of financial success but recognizes that success covers many aspects of life other than just the financial side. The principles discussed here apply equally to success in any of life's endeavors. One aspect of my life that gives me great joy is the success of my two sons. While they were growing up, I shared with them the principles expressed in this book. Each took those principles and folded them into their own lives with great success. Each is successful in his career, and each has a warm and loving family. Both are honest, hardworking, and caring people. This book talks about the three areas I consider important for obtaining and enjoying success. They are attitude, goal setting, and planning. Each will be discussed as separate topics.

I have presented my thoughts on success in story format simply because I think it will be more interesting. In the story, I am Mr. Thomas and his thoughts are my thoughts. Come along now as Mr. Thomas and his young friend share the joy of learning.

1
THE MEETING

I WILL ALWAYS REMEMBER OUR FIRST MEETING. IT WAS THE SUMMER OF 1956. I had just graduated from high school and was two weeks away from my first full-time job. The job interview had gone well, partly because I convinced the interviewer that I was a quick learner. The work was making large cables used in aircraft simulators for the purpose of training new pilots. I wanted to be an engineer of some kind and thought this was as close as I could come. Engineers need at least some college and I had none. I had a burning desire to go to college, but no idea how that could ever happen. Back then, there was no such thing as government-backed student loans. College was on my mind that June afternoon as I strolled through my neighborhood park. I soon found a bench and decided to sit for a while and think about the future. There was an elderly gentleman already sitting there. And as I sat, we exchanged head nods and I quickly went into deep thought. After a short time, the gentleman spoke, "Pardon me, young man."

I simply responded, "Yes?" as I turned and visually took him in. He was neatly dressed in a well-tailored blue shirt and a summer weight sweater of a lighter blue. His trousers were black and casually styled. His face was friendly and warm, and his hair was a wonderful silver-white with every hair in place.

He introduced himself, "My name is Fred Thomas, and I am sorry to interrupt but you seem to be very deep in thought for one so young. Would you like to talk?"

Sharing my concerns seemed to be a good idea. So, I began. I told him of my desire to become successful, financially well-off, and to obtain a college degree. He asked why I wanted a degree and I expressed my desire to become an engineer. Mr. Thomas gave me a knowing smile and said, "I have been around a few years and consider myself successful. I would be happy to pass along my thoughts on success if you would be interested."

At that point in my life, I was willing to take all the help I could get, and I told him so. He said it would take more than a few hours of conversation, and so we struck a deal. We would meet as often as we could. And if I reached a point where I felt there was no more to be gained, we would end the meetings with no hard feelings. That first two weeks before I started work, we met a total of five times. Once I started working, we only met a few hours on Saturdays and occasionally on Sundays after church. When Fred arrived before me, I often found him reading from a little red book. When he saw me approaching, he would put the book into his pocket and greet me in his usual warm manner. I admit I had curiosity about the book but figured if he wanted me to know about it, he would tell me. It turned out I was right. At one of our meetings, he seemed to become aware of my curiosity and willingly shared. He said the book contained definitions of success by many famous people. It also contained phrases and words he often used as motivational touchstones. There were word definitions and numbers related to success that he often referred to. He promised to make me a copy for my own reference and one I could add to as my own experiences unfolded.

2
ATTITUDE

Mr. Thomas said the three main elements to achieving success are attitude, goal setting, and a plan. Separately, they are a dynamic reality. Combined, they are an amazing force. He suggested we take a close look at the three elements. He said we should start by looking at attitude because he considered it the number one factor for success.

First, how is success defined? Fred quoted the famous leadership manager, Paul J. Meyer as saying, "Success is the progressive realization of predetermined, worthwhile personal goals." Notice, this does not specifically mention financial success. It allows for goals unrelated to financial success. These include such ideas as family life, personal relationships, and educational achievements. The simplest definition is "the achievement of a goal."

Many people think of money and success together. Some say money cannot buy happiness, and my experience causes me to agree. A person may be wealthy but might not be happy because of a miserable family life. An individual may have many goals, success in one does not guarantee success in the others. Mr. Thomas promised when we finished our talks, I would be ready to plan for success, commit to it, and get on the path to achieving it. I said it all sounded so simple. He said in principle it is but it requires dedication and commitment, and that requires action. Without action, the plan is only a fantasy. He continued by pointing out that success has its own attitude. Any person with a bad attitude who acquires success will find that success short-lived. Attitudes about success and money break down into three parts: how society feels about success and money, how you feel about success, and your attitude about deserving success.

3

SOCIETY'S ATTITUDE ABOUT SUCCESS

Mr. Thomas told me that since success is something most people work toward, you would think they would admire and support those who are successful, but that is often not the case. He said your friends want you to be successful, just not too successful. Friends are often like you in thought and spirit. Your success makes them look bad or feel bad about themselves. Many people resent successful people. They may think a successful person must be dishonest, a backstabber, or have inherited wealth and/or privilege that was not earned or deserved. They often feel a successful person becomes a snob who can no longer be bothered with them. To them, it seems that becoming successful or obtaining a position of rank changes a person. The successful person appears to stop associating with old friends or even family members. The real reason for less association is the ability of the successful person to do financially what the others cannot. One might be able to travel the world in search of adventure while the other cannot.

I interrupted to ask whether that meant if I became successful, would I lose friends? He said it was possible for friends to remain close but drifting apart is most likely. A good relationship can remain intact if each person appreciates the other for who they are and not where they are on the social or financial ladder. People often feel success has changed their friend. They say it must be true, "Success and money corrupt." This is as an excuse frequently used for not putting in the required effort for success.

I believe money only allows people to be more of what they were before the money came. If a person was caring and sharing before having money, they will be the same after earning it. The person who was egotistical and shellfish before the money is more-so afterward. As Billy Graham once said, "There is nothing wrong with men possessing riches. The wrong comes when riches possess men." Life is better with more options and money provides just that. Henry Ford never owned a Cadillac, but he had the option. It is one thing to drive an economy car because you want to, and another because you must.

By this time in our acquaintance, autumn was approaching and we started meeting at a local coffee shop. It seemed like no time had passed before Christmas arrived. By then, I had become comfortable calling Mr. Thomas, Fred, and we had become good friends. I enjoyed his warm and caring attitude and his willingness to share his knowledge. His respect and interest in my opinion gave me a sense of self-worth. On Fred's part, I think he enjoyed my youth and my expectations about all that life has to offer. Over time, we shared more about ourselves and our families.

I told Fred I was from Virginia. I talked about my mom, my dad, and my high school years. Fred was from New Mexico, and his son and daughter still lived there. He founded a consulting firm in New Mexico, and several years later moved to Virginia to be close to his government clients in Washington, D.C. Fred's son was the head of human resources for a defense contractor, and his daughter was a contract lawyer.

Christmas was a very enjoyable time for us that year. Our little coffee shop had morphed into a warm and comfortable living Christmas card. The windows played home to crystal frost in the corners while the small fireplace offered its magical glow. All the while, a tree in the corner told its own seasonal story.

We sat in the charm of the little coffee shop and passed the time talking about our families and our Christmas traditions. We even exchanged gifts. Fred had indicated at an earlier meeting that he wanted to learn more about meditation so I gave him a recorded lecture on the subject. He gave me a book, *Think and Grow Rich*, by Napoleon Hill. He said it was one of the most famous motivational books ever written. In giving it to me, he reminded me that our discussions were about success and not about getting rich. He said that even though the book was about acquiring wealth, it contained much wisdom on becoming successful.

In fulfillment of his promise, he also gave me a copy of his little red book. He encouraged me to add my own thoughts and motivations to it.

The season was one of love and sharing with friends and family. After Christmas, we started talking about the blending of society's attitude on success and my own. I found the subject fascinating since I had never given it any thought.

4
YOU AND SOCIETY'S ATTITUDES

Since you are part of society, let us look at how society's thoughts about success might influence you. People often make the mistake of asking the wrong people for advice. Fred told me that when he started out, he had many of the questions I have about success. He began looking for answers and found few of his friends had any. He came to realize only a few of his successful friends had answers and, amazingly, they were happy to share.

Those friends knew about achieving success because they had already done it. Fred said that was the lesson; do not waste time asking questions of people unqualified to answer them. Unless your brother-in-law who is an auto mechanic was once an astronaut, why ask him about how to become one? Unless your barber or hair stylist has made money marketing their invention, why ask them how to market yours? This is exactly what too many people do. They seek advice from those unqualified to give it. They just give up their dreams based on the opinions of those unskilled in advising them. Worse, they accept those answers as facts and base the potential for future success on them. Here is a good suggestion from Michelle Rutz, Business Development Director: "If people are doubting how far you can go, go so far that you can't hear them anymore."

One aspect that is seldom discussed about success is just being a nice person. Do people see you as someone they can trust? John Lennon once said, "Being honest may not get you lots of friends, but it'll always get you the right ones."

Are you seen as a person who seeks a win-win solution in negotiations? It is often said, "Nice guys always finish last." Fred explained that his experience had been just the opposite. I would say about fifty percent of my success, both personally and professionally, has been based on my ability to get along with people. It never hurts to be as diplomatic as possible. Remember, words have meaning and power. Words carry emotion. Chose them carefully. Everyone thinks of themselves as the most important person in the room. It is essential to remember that when interacting with them. When you treat people with respect and reaffirm their importance, they will respond in kind. If you think you know it all, you may be surprised to know that you do not! There are plenty of things you do not know. Luckily, the people who know what you do not know are happy to share if you treat them with kindness and respect.

I have known several individuals over the years who aspired to be managers. They had all the qualifications needed except one. When working with people, their attitude was very abrasive. One of these individuals was a handsome man with clear, penetrating eyes. His voice was a smooth baritone, except when he became demanding. Then it was threatening like a locomotive bearing down. He was assigned to lead a team seeking to acquire funding for a research project. One day, he introduced an approach to the problem and announced it would be the one the team would use. One team member said she did not understand why that approach was best. She was told it did not matter if she understood, only that she followed it. You can imagine how unwilling the team was to follow his direction after that. Those not working well with others and not treating others with respect seldom go beyond the very beginning levels of management.

Fred continued with another story. Lee Iacocca, former head of the Chrysler Corporation was to address a convention of Chrysler dealers and no one was sure what the subject would be. It turned out to be about increasing sales. He said the secret was to make someone like you. His point was that all car brands are well made, attractive, and generally cover the same price range. So why would someone buy from one manufacturer over another? His answer was because the car shopper likes one businessperson over another. Since Iacocca was talking to business people about work, let us talk about work.

Fred asked about my attitude about work. That question is not about work in general, but about work specifically. "Is it something you feel you must do, or something you enjoy doing? It is said that when a person does work that is enjoyed, it is not like work at all. I generally agree with that, but believe me," Fred continued, "there will be days when remembering that is hard. Enjoying what you do is important. It is a sad story when people reach their senior years with unfulfilled longings of what could have been."

Fred began a new story by saying that a good friend of his worked for the Social Security Agency and for many years would tell him stories of people applying for aid. So many of these people had tales of regret.

One man told him that when he was younger, he really wanted to be a commercial artist. His wife insisted he go into the family clothing business working for her father. He put aside his dreams and did what she wanted. The man acknowledged the work had given him security and a good living. However, he said he always regretted never pursuing his passion for art. At the time he shared his story, his sight was so bad he was no longer able to make his dream happen.

Another story involved a remarkably successful gentleman who owned his own business. As he filed for retirement, he told of how he had poured his life into building that business. He did not spend much time with his two sons as they were growing up. Now, both were married and had children of their own. And ironically, they had little time outside of their own families to spend with their father. This last story is an example of being successful in one area of life, but not in another.

5

EDUCATION

I came to one of our meetings filled with excitement and Fred recognized it right away. He asked what had gotten into me. I explained I just found out the company I worked for had a college tuition refund program. I would be required to pay for courses myself; however, so long as I earned a "B" or higher, the company would reimburse me. That meant I would be able to afford college.

Fred was happy for me but not surprised my company offered such a plan. He said it was a great employee benefit and was surprised I was not told about it when I was offered the job. He said a reimbursement program was one of the best ways to pay for college. He went so far as to say when looking for a job with all things being equal, go with the company offering such plans. That would be true even if you already had a degree. You might decide to earn a higher degree or specialize in a specific area. There is always room to improve your understanding of the work you are currently doing.

Fred continued, "A reimbursement program is great but not the only one that helps with obtaining a higher education. People in military service can often take college courses. The military also has special savings plans designed to help members pay for college after enlistment is over. Anyone going to one of the military academies

(Army, Navy, Air Force, Coast Guard, or Merchant Marines) will receive a four-year degree in exchange for several years of service." Many colleges and universities offer credit for real-life experiences. This is done by exams or other forms of written work that demonstrate life experiences equal to the course offered by the specific institution. For example, a divorced person could write a paper about the experience and receive credit from a college offering a course in home and family life.

Many schools in some states offer college credit by examination. A passing grade indicates the applicant possesses the equivalent knowledge offered by a college course.

Further, there are many scholarships offered which are not always based on grades alone. Many states offer full or partial reimbursement of tuition if the student studies a particular profession and agrees to work for the state in that profession for a specified length of time. Becoming a teacher would be an example of such a program.

Continuing, Fred said there are a few correspondence schools that offer degrees. He then concluded that anyone could get a degree if they are willing to do the work required to earn one.

Fred would be amazed that correspondence schools have mainly been replaced by universities offering online degree programs. He would also be surprised at the extensive use of student loans. The widespread use of student loans has proven Fred's wisdom when he told me, "Debt always reduces the options available to you." Take an example of a young married couple, both with large outstanding student loan balances. They might have to put off buying a home because their education loans prevent them from qualifying for a loan.

Fred took on a serious tone and began a discussion about the importance of courses offered as electives. He said many students just consider them courses to get out of the way, but they are much more than that. They can be the foundation of a well-rounded education. For example, if you become an engineer, it is important to speak the language of engineering but there is another social world outside of work. The people in that world want to talk about books, current events, or a vast number of topics. They are not interested in the stress points of the bridge you are designing. College should teach you how to think, not what to think. When you leave school, you should not only have a career path but also a broad education. These are not the same.

6
SELF ATTITUDE

As usual, our next meeting started off with Fred and me catching up on the past week of activities. Then Fred started talking about personal attitude. He began by saying a person's attitude about themselves is the biggest difference between being wonderfully successful, moderately successful, or depressingly unsuccessful. Once a person has the right attitude, it is no longer a question of whether they will become successful, but rather how soon it will happen.

Fred's opinion was that to be successful, you must believe you can be, and that you deserve to be. Those ideas may seem to be the same but they are not. Many people know they can be successful and many almost make it. They fall short because they do not feel they deserve it. Famous American comedian Lucille Ball once said, "Love yourself first and everything else fall into line. You really have to love yourself to get anything done in this world."

Fred said, "For now, let us look at the attitude that matters most, your attitude about yourself. If a person's self-image is one of low self-esteem, it will need adjustment to achieve success. High achievement and low self-esteem do not play well together. The number of people with low self-esteem who sabotage their drive toward success is amazing."

I interrupted Fred to ask, "Why would anyone sabotage their own activities?"

Fred told me that many people simply do not believe they deserve success. An example would be the person who is asked to give a speech and that speech could have an enormously positive impact on the speaker's future. They practice and practice the speech but when the moment arrives, they get nervous and blow it. It is not a conscious act but one that will repeat itself over and over again. The feeling of unworthiness may have come from many sources. The opinion of others may have imprinted images of unworthiness on the brain. It is most devastating if it came from parents or those whose opinion is admired above all others.

Fred told a story about training elephants. Tie a baby elephant's leg to a stake using a small rope. The baby is so young it is unable to break the rope. When it grows up, it will not even try to break the rope because when young, it was conditioned to believe it could not. The lesson, Fred said, is that this is often the case with people. Early training conditions people to believe there are limits that do not really exist. Limitations can often affect large groups of people, not just individuals. For decades, there was a psychological barrier that no one could run a mile in less than four minutes. Many tried and failed. This led to the widespread belief that the human body's construction prevented it from reaching a faster speed. Then, in 1954, a young runner named Roger Bannister ran a mile in 3 minutes, 59.4 seconds. The interesting lesson is that within a year of the limit being broken, four other runners ran the mile in less than four minutes. The moral is be careful of limits others may try to put on you.

Fred commented that many times parents pass on negative attitudes about successful or wealthy people and those can create limits in the mind of a child. It is possible to spot people with low self-esteem by one trait. They often sabotage their own progress within one or two steps from reaching their goal. They drop out of college just short of completing their degree; they do not tie the ends of the afghan they knitted; or they do not write the last chapter of their book. If they did finish their project, they would be faced with having done something of value and their low self-esteem would not allow for that. They also can have plenty of reasons why they could not finish. If it were a real reason, there would be a real solution.

Fred was reminded of an answer given by the advice columnist Ann Landers. Someone had asked her, "I am thinking about going to college but it will take me six years and when I finish, I will be in my mid-fifties. Do you think I will be too old?" The answer was, "How old will you be in six years if you do not go to college?" Everyone has within them unrealized potential, and for many, it will never be realized because of fear of failure or fear of rejection.

Almost to himself, Fred commented, "I have never had low self-esteem." Then he continued, "I am amazed how anyone can disregard the wonder of being a unique human being. There never existed, nor will there ever exist, anyone like you. You have talents and gifts that totally belong to you and no one else. From the moment of conception, you were successful and unique.

"There were thousands and thousands of sperm competing to fertilize an egg and you won. At that moment you defeated thousands and thousands of competitors in the race of a lifetime. You were born unique. So keep this in mind, society survives on conformity but advances only on uniqueness. Society will attempt to push you through the funnel of conformance starting in infancy. You will be dressed in the color corresponding to your sex: pink for girls, blue for boys. You will attend a school offering a set program of learning and then you may or may not attend college. Conforming to society's thinking, attending college would be the best choice. You will be expected to own a home, a car, get married, and have 2.5 children. Society leaves it up to you how you work out the .5 child. It is expected that you will retire around age sixty-five and after that not make too many waves while waiting for your time to run out.

"This is conformity but what about uniqueness? You were born unique and that means you have something to contribute. I do not know what makes you unique. I only know you are. Maybe you do not have many answers but lots of questions; society needs those as much as it needs answers. As Albert Einstein once said, 'I have no special talent, I am only passionately curious.' He also said, 'The important thing is not to stop questioning. Curiosity has its own reason for existence.'"

Look at the gifts we possess at birth. They include sight, hearing, touch, smell, and taste. If one of our senses is missing, our astonishing brain provides us with the means to compensate for the loss. Regarding the five senses and our amazing bodies, we have miles of nerve endings that detect the smallest rain drop. On a warm summer evening we feel the breeze as gentle as a baby's touch. Our sense of smell allows us to detect the warning signs of acid, smelling smoke, or the tantalizing smell of jasmine. The sensors in our eyes are so refined that they detect hundreds of shades of color. Our vision allows us to notice the minute movement of the smallest bird in a forest of trees. Our hearing allows us to travel and never move. We can soar to the mountains on the sounds of a symphony orchestra. We can float away on a cloud as we listen to the peaceful babbling of a nearby stream. We can taste a cherry right from the tree or the multiple flavors of a home-cooked meal. Our brains are so far above the ability of a computer. It is like the difference between the speed of a bullet and that of a snail. Processing information into a computer requires written or verbal input. We, on the other hand, receive large amounts of input simply by holding another's hand. That act conveys a sensation of caring, companionship, warmth, and trust. These are feelings completely missed by a computer. Scientists around the world are trying to teach computers to do what our brains do automatically thousands of times a day. No other creature on earth has the logic or creativity of a human.

If you live in a free democracy, you do not need permission to be successful. Ben Steverman, on November 21, 2016, *Bloomberg Report*, wrote, "Every day the United States of America produces 1700 millionaires." It is possible for you to become one too, if that is what you want. The key phrase in that sentence is, "If that is what you want."

Let yourself understand it is okay if that is not what you want. If you want it, it comes with a lot of hard work, pressure, and sacrifice. The point is that you live in a country where it is possible. In most advanced cultures some education is provided. The United States provides free education through high school. College education is obtainable but it may take hard work and planning. Remember, food is available for the birds but it is not available in the nest. They must work for it. To feel unworthy or have low self-esteem, a person must ignore the array of gifts they possess and the opportunities they are given.

Fred said, "When you meet those people, tell them to stop ignoring those gifts. Stop ignoring their uniqueness. Take stock of blessings. Today, start making your plans for success. Join those of us who believe in natural talents and work to make the most of yours."

7
ATTITUDE ABOUT WORK

Fred started one of our meeting by saying success and work are intertwined. However, the only place "success" comes before "work" is in the dictionary. The good news is success does not require mind-numbing work or back-breaking labor. It only requires ten percent more. Ten percent more time, effort, and study will put you way ahead of your associates. If you are a student wanting to be at the upper level of your classes, put in ten percent more. If you have an assignment requiring two hours, put in two hours and twelve minutes. If you work a 9 to 5 job, put in an extra four hours per week. Do these things, and be amazed at the success that comes your way. That ten percent extra will bring you the recognition you want and deserve.

If you have your sights set on becoming wealthy, the ten percent figure goes out the window. You are looking at something more like 12-hour days for three to five years. There are only two sources for generating money. One is people at work. The other is money at work. In the beginning of striving for wealth, most of the earnings will come from your own work efforts. The more success you have, the more earnings can come from money at work.

Many admire the success and accomplishments of others but few are willing to do the extra work required to reach the level they so admire. I am reminded of a story told by Ann Landers that is a great example of this point.

A group of ladies would meet every other week for a book club. One week, they decided to forego the usual meeting and have a luncheon with music. The music would be provided by a well-known local pianist. The luncheon went well and the music was outstanding. The pianist played pop, classical, and show tunes. When she finished, there was a nice round of applause. Then one of the ladies called out from her table, "I would give anything to play the piano the way you do." The pianist shocked the room by responding, "If you believe that, you are lying to yourself." The room got as quiet as falling snow. The pianist went on to explain, "If you practiced two hours a day, six days a week as I do, if you memorized hundreds of pages of sheet music, as I have done, and if you paid thousands of dollars to great teachers, as I do, then, you might be better than I am. When you say you would give anything, you simply do not mean it. Many who admire the accomplishments of others are not willing to put in the time and effort to reach the level they so admire. That is where commitment comes in. If you are committed to success, you must be willing to do what it takes to acquire it."

8
ATTITUDE ABOUT FEAR

FRED ASKED, "DO YOU THINK MOST PEOPLE'S ATTITUDE IS AFFECTED by fear?" I said I had never really thought about it. He went on, "Maybe that is because fear is not usually associated with an attitude. When discussing an attitude for success, it is a factor to be considered. A great many people have a fear of failure. They fear the embarrassment it will cause them. They fear they will lose the respect of friends and loved ones. They fear their hopes and dreams will be destroyed by failure. You will note in every case, it is the loss of self-image that causes fear."

Fred continued, "During the Great Depression of the 1930's, Americans feared not having money for food, clothing, and shelter...the necessities of life. Amid this background, Franklin Roosevelt was elected president. In his inaugural speech he said, 'We have nothing to fear but fear itself.' He realized that fear could immobilize action and hold back action to solve the Great Depression."

The dictionary defines fear as an emotion aroused by impending danger, real or imagined. Imagined fear is the one that affects success. Robert Iger, former CEO of Disney for 15 years, said, "Fear can delay or prevent making decisions that can affect the individual and the organization." He went on to say, "There can be no innovation if you operate out of a fear of the new."

If you make a decision that has a negative result, it is important that fear does not prevent or slow you down from making a corrective decision. I have a theory I want to share. I do not believe the average person ever makes the wrong decision; let me explain. When a person selects one of the many possible solutions to a problem, it is based on available information. No normal, rational, thinking person would evaluate the options and deliberately pick one thought to be wrong. They would pick the best one based on the information they have. Do not misunderstand me, decisions often have negative or unforeseen results. That does not mean the decision was wrong. It means it was based on incorrect or missing information, or bad assumptions. Negative results only mean a new decision is required. Life always presents unexpected setbacks. Success does not depend on how many times you get knocked down, but on how many times you get back up.

9
ATTITUDE ABOUT FAILURE

Fred believed strongly that no one should fear failure. He said if you do not stumble, it is because you are standing still and not moving ahead. Each failure should be viewed as a great opportunity to learn. You will always learn more from your failures than your successes. Thomas Edison once said, "I am very well educated. I know thousands of things that do not work."

To handle a failure, examine it, learn from it, work to discover why it happened and how to prevent it from happening again. Then, move on. The only reason ever to revisit a failure is to discuss what you learned from it. In personal and business relationships, it is more important to find a solution to a problem than to find someone to blame. After the solution is discovered, there is time to figure out where the cause lies. If a person or group of people are found to be the cause of failure then that problem needs to be addressed.

10
WORDS HAVE POWER

From our very first meeting, I was impressed with Fred's vocabulary and use of language. His words were well-chosen and precisely conveyed his thoughts. I was not surprised when Fred told me, "You may not be aware, but people partly judge you by your vocabulary. The better it is, the better educated you are presumed to be."

He continued, "Verbal communication requires a minimum of two people: a speaker and a listener. The speaker puts forth a series of words. Those words are heard by the listener. Then comes the tricky part. The listener must interpret the meaning of the words. The more precise the words, the more likely a correct interpretation will result." A warning of caution: the words used should not be so sophisticated as to be beyond the listener's vocabulary. Instructions and directions should be given in the simplest words that covey exact meaning.

"There are approximately a million words in the English language. How many of them do you use in daily language? Vocabulary can be a factor in success, and lucky for us all, it is an area where improvement is possible. We can all learn by listening to others. When you hear a word you are not familiar with, ask the speaker for the meaning. I sense your fear of embarrassment at the idea of doing this.

Adding a new word to your vocabulary is worth a momentary embarrassment.

"It turns out your teachers were right. If you do not know the meaning of a word, look it up. It will be worth your time. As soon as you can, use the new word in a sentence and often in conversation. That will reinforce it in your mind. Remember, the larger your vocabulary, the better you can communicate."

Words not only convey thoughts, they also carry and create emotions. Realizing this will help create friends, followers, supporters, and lovers. The incorrectly chosen word can embarrass or discourage. The carefully chosen word can motivate and encourage. "You screwed up," and "You made a mistake," carry the same meaning but not the same emotional impact. The right word at the right moment can win or lose a friend, supporter, or a negotiation.

The following are a few additional examples:

1a. "If you need help with your project, call on me." This is an offer of help. It is a commitment to act if needed.

1b. "If you start your project, I support you one-hundred percent." This is not a commitment of action and promises nothing.

2a. If you say, "I will do it," that is a commitment to do whatever it takes to accomplish the goal.

2b. If you say, "I can do it," that implies the ability or the willingness to acquire the ability to complete the task.

2c. If you say, "I cannot do it," that is a cop-out. The person who says this is saying, "I am unwilling to take the time and make the effort to do it." Most average people can achieve most things they are willing to commit to doing.

Each example might be interpreted differently by the listener. If there is any doubt, ask for clarification. If you are not sure you understood what was said, repeat what you heard and ask if that is what was meant. A conversation requires two people: a listener and a speaker.

They exchange roles as the conversation goes on. There really are two listeners and one speaker at any given time. This is because the speaker is also listening to what is being spoken. This is important because your mind hears and records what you are saying. One of the brain's functions is to record and play back the main ideas presented to it. The brain records what your senses input. It makes no judgment on the accuracy of the data. When you say to someone, "I am not good at math," the brain records it as fact. Later, when faced with a math problem, your brain will remind you of what you said about your math ability. Words have power.

Be careful what you say about yourself when speaking to others. Your brain is recording what you say and its feedback helps define who you are and who you become.

We have been discussing being an accurate speaker. Let us now discuss being a good listener. Being a good listener requires effort and concentration. Listening shows interest and people are impressed when you show that you are interested in them and their opinions. Good listening requires concentration. Practice maintaining focus. Do not let your mind wander. When people speak, the exact meaning of what is heard is often different from what was intended. That is why you need to stay focused and watch for facial expression and body language.

Listen to determine if the structure of the sentence fits the content of the subject being discussed. Be alert when the speaker says one thing but implies another. When you learn to listen, you will often hear what is not said. This is referred to as reading between the lines, and it takes practice.

11

OPTIONS

During one of our meetings, Fred started talking about options. He said he could not imagine anything worse than facing one of life's challenges with only one option available. He declared the most important aspect of a successful life is maintaining options.

An option is the power or right of choosing. One thing that reduces options quickly is debt. The closer you are to being debt free, the more options you will have. You can travel more, donate more, and enjoy a better quality of life.

Having options applies to the whole family. It is one reason you should encourage your children to do well in school. Children with good grades and who have a broad exposure to a variety of extracurricular activities have more options to advance their learning beyond high school. They have a wider range of options regarding career path, whatever that path may be. They have more options about how to achieve those goals, especially when it concerns scholarships, student loans, and work/study programs that may be needed to specialize and pursue work-place happiness.

Many such options are not available to students with low grades. The range of colleges that will accept them is reduced. If their grades are too low, they may not be accepted at all without first taking remedial classes. Paying for college is a greater problem for them. There are no academic scholarships available to them. Loans are harder to get. The jobs available to them are more menial and pay less.

Your level and type of education can affect your life options. If you have a master's degree and decide to be a carpenter, that option is yours but you also have plenty of other options.

If you never finished high school, working as a clerk or in a trade may be your only option. Even your area of study in college will affect your career options. Study communications and many career options are open to you. Major in history and your options are reduced. The options you envision for yourself should be considered when constructing your goals and plans. What type of career are you looking for? What kind of house or car do you want? What steps in your planning will help you manifest these outcomes? Your options regarding retirement will depend on the options you chose during your working years.

12
GOAL SETTING

"When I got cut from the varsity team as a sophomore in high school, I learned something. I knew I never wanted to feel that bad again. I never wanted to have that taste in my mouth, that hole in my stomach. So I set a goal of becoming a starter on the varsity."
—Michael Jordan, professional basketball player.

Fred offered a definition of a goal and then expanded on it. A goal is an idea of the future, or a desired result that a person or group of people envision, plan, and commit to achieve. Goals are associated with timelines for completion.

This definition contains several key words. The first is envision. It is essential that a person visualize the desired goal. Conceiving is the first step. If the same thought or image is fed to the mind again and again, the mind accepts it as fact and starts to provide ideas to support that reality. The mind makes no judgement between fact and fiction. It simply accepts what you put in as factual data.

An example would be if you tell your brain you are 6' tall, but in reality you are only 5' 8", your brain will accept the 6' assumption, but if you instantly think, *I am only 5'8"*, the brain then accepts the latest data input as fact. It has no way to physically measure your height. It only knows what you input. It is the same when telling your brain what you want to achieve and acting as if you have achieved it. The mind accepts it as fact and starts providing ideas to support the belief. We will come back to this point in the section on planning. For now, let us look at the second important word in the definition: plans.

Plans are the specific steps to be taken in achieving the goal. Just like goals, they need to be written down. They are specific and time related. The third word of importance in the definition is commitment. Commitment is the difference between "I wish I had" and "I have." Wishing requires no action; commitment involves work. When you commit, you are agreeing to do whatever it takes to reach the goal. This might mean getting more education or retraining. It might require an attitude adjustment such as being more outgoing or working outside your comfort zone. Arthur Ashe, the great tennis champion, said of success, "One important key to success is self-confidence. An important key to self-confidence is preparation."

A commitment is an agreement with yourself to work through the failures and mistakes you will make on your way to success.

Goals are what motivate us to action. Goals are like magnets pulling us into the future we desire. They are the things we strive for, the targets upon which we set out sights. Selecting a goal is critical. The correctly selected goal creates within us a burning desire to achieve it. It is the goal, and the desire it creates, that will cause us to do the extra ten percent. It will cause us to study one more hour, make one more call, reach down and pull out that extra reserve of energy.

It is important that you answer for yourself some specific questions: do you want to work for someone else or for yourself? If for someone else, what kind of job do you want, and what do you want from that job? What are you going to give to your family? What do you want for your health and what are you willing to give to reach that goal? These and similar questions need to be asked and answered before writing and committing to your goals.

Realize the acquisition of money is seldom a goal in itself. If it is, you should reevaluate your values. It is not money, but the things money can acquire and help to achieve that should motivate. When setting a goal for money, it should be based on the future cost of the items you are seeking or lifestyle you wish to create.

Money is not just for acquiring things. It can also do a lot to help others. Goals provide an image to the mind. Imagine what you can do when your money exceeds your needs. Can your mind envision future generations obtaining college degrees because of the foundation you established? Think of the people who your money could assist when donated to your favored charities. Goal setting is not something to be taken lightly. It requires a lot of thought. As the old saying goes, "Be careful what you wish for; it might come true." This reminds me of a joke about a man who finds a magic lamp, rubs it, and a genie appears. The genie asks the man what his wish is and the man says he wants to be a real stud. Just like that, the man became a rivet in a snow tire in Montana during a blizzard.

Goals should be written down and read aloud twice a day. This reading will imbed itself in your brain. Thinking about your goals will become automatic. Ask yourself what you need to help reach each step in your goal. Do you need increased knowledge, the help of others, or specific tools? Acquiring these items in a timely manner is part of the plan.

13
COMMITMENT

Fred reminded me that we had talked about commitment as part of goal setting. He reviewed the dictionary definition as "a state or quality of being dedicated to a cause or activity. A pledge or undertaking." He then pointed out that there are two words so strongly associated with commitment as to be inseparable. They are "perseverance" and "persistence." Perseverance is defined as a continued effort to do or achieve something despite difficulties, failure, or opposition. He again reminded me that there would be plenty of those.

A fine example of perseverance is a baby learning to walk. First comes standing. Babies usually start by holding on to something and pulling themselves up. That is followed by falling and pulling up again. That is repeated until falling disappears from the process. Next comes walking, usually a few steps from one adult to another. That process also includes trying and falling, trying and falling again until falling stops occurring. Walking then becomes running, and running becomes chasing. Notice that nowhere in the process does the baby become embarrassed by falling. Unlike adults, they do not look around to see if someone saw them fail. They do not compare their efforts to the efforts of other babies. Those seem to be traits we develop on our way to becoming adults. Babies do not seem to care about their failures or what others think about those failures. They ignore them and keep going until they achieve success.

Persistence is the act of doing something for a long, or longer than usual length of time. No better example exists than the following:

Event	Age
Failed in business	22
Ran for US Legislature-defeated	23
Again failed in business	24
Elected to US Legislature	25
Sweetheart dies	26
Nervous breakdown	27
Defeated for Speaker of the House	29
Defeated for Presidential Elector	31
Defeated for US Congress	34
Elected to US Congress	37
Defeated for US Senate	46
Defeated for US Vice President	47
Elected US President, Abraham Lincoln	51

14

MAKING AND FOLLOWING PLANS

AT WHAT WOULD BE OUR LAST MEETING, FRED TOOK UP THE SUBJECT of making and following plans. Summarizing his thoughts, he said, "It is not enough just to have a goal. You must have a plan to reach your goal. Remember, hope is not a strategy. The goal is what you desire. The plan is a written statement of how and when you will reach the goal, and what you are willing to trade to reach it. Remember also, if you do not have a plan for success, you automatically have a plan for failure. Most people never reach a high level of financial freedom simply because they have no plan to get there. If you want to test this theory, ask the next ten people you meet how much they plan to be earning at the end of the next five years, the next ten years, and then ask how they plan to reach that income.

"You will be surprised how few have any specific plan at all. Most people simply go along and settle for far less than they are worth. Their plan, if you can call it that, is just get a job at a specified amount, take the annual raise as it comes or does not come, and someday retire. For that reason, the person who has a plan for success is already ahead of the crowd.

"It is this lack of planning that accounts for ninety-five percent of people reaching retirement age and being partially dependent on the government, friends, or relatives for financial support. Yes! It is amazing but true. In this country of great freedoms and opportunities, only about five percent ever reach the financial independence we all talk about. The difference between talking about it and planning for it is that talking does not get the job done. Talking is easy but planning takes work. And I assure you, if you are not willing to work, you will never achieve success.

"To be effective, plans need to be written down, read, and reread until they become imprinted in your mind. Plans should include short, medium, and long-term objectives. The short-term plans should be extremely detailed. They should be so detailed as to provide a step-by-step process and schedule to reach them. Even though these plans are detailed, they need to be flexible enough to allow for modification, because unexpected events will occur. The unexpected events will prove the value of the planning. It will be the plan that puts you back on track when the unexpected knocks you off. Short-term planning should be aimed at reaching short-term goals. Each goal should be designed as a step toward the long-term goal. Each step of the plan should have a set time for completion. Remember, no calendar has a someday.

"One path to success is to associate with successful people. In trying to learn how to become successful, look to people who have proven they know how.

"Aristotle Onassis, the great shipping magnate worth 500 million dollars, was asked if he lost it all, how would he start over. His answer, "I would find a way to be around successful people." You would not ask a fast-food worker how to extract a tooth, so why ask him how to become a dentist? Why ask a store clerk how to become wealthy? If the clerk knew how to be wealthy, he would be. I cannot even imagine how many success stories have been squashed by seeking advice from someone unqualified to give it. That is the kind of mistake people make.

"Too many people buy into the wrong type of advice and allow it to steal their dreams. If you believe someone has pointed out a real problem, fix it and go forward with your dream. Get educated, change your appearance, make and follow your plan, and hang out with people who share and believe in your dream. Success takes effort. If you are standing still, you are falling behind and just do not know it.

"The standing still concept also applies to education. You should always be learning. Some people get a college education and try to stretch that education over a lifetime. That does not work. People, things, and situations change. Changes require changing knowledge. The attainment of success requires staying focused on the goal. The plan is your aid to staying focused. When decisions are needed, a review of the plan allows you to focus on decisions that move you toward, rather than away from your goal.

"Focus requires awareness, awareness of the conversations, thoughts, and emotions of the moment. A large percentage of decisions are based on emotions, and that can cause lack of focus. How many times have you needed to do something but chose what you wanted to do more? Some of this comes from our stone age ancestors who survived by relying on emotions. The stone age generation acted out of fear and satisfaction. These are emotional and not logical responses.

"Today, when a decision needs to be made, emotions often win out. As an example, say you walk past a bakery and see a wonderful looking eclair in the window. You imagine how good it would taste so you go in and buy it. That is an emotional desire. The logical part of the brain reacts a little slower than the emotional part. With a slight delay on your part, the logical brain would have kicked in and helped you realize that the eclair can lead to weight gain, cause a sugar overload, or help you understand that you were not really hungry at all.

"Emotions can easily kidnap conversations when focus is lost. Here is an example. A husband and wife are discussing what major area of study their son should pursue in college. The husband thinks he should study engineering like his grandfather. The wife favors a musical major. Everything is going well until the wife says, 'Engineering! What did that ever do for your father?' The wife, most likely without realizing it, just interjected emotion into a logical conversation. One or both people need to be aware of what just happened and redirect the conversation back to the subject being discussed. The emotional part of our brain moves quicker than the logical part. When making an important decision, allow a little more time before deciding and allow the logical brain a chance to catch up."

Earlier I said I would never forget when Fred and I first met. The same is true of the last meeting we had before he moved away. It was in our little coffee shop in the early part of spring. It was not yet warm enough to meet outside but in the air was the delightful promise of warmer weather.

I arrived first with no idea what was to come. When Fred arrived there was something different. The smile was not as bright and there were a few wrinkles in his forehead. He looked like he had a thought to share but did not know where to begin. As soon as he sat down, I said, "Fred, what is the matter?"

The wrinkles seemed to vanish and he said, "I will get right to the point. Over the last number of months my health has been declining and I have decided to move back to New Mexico to be near family." He said, "I have been thinking a lot about our seasons and decided I have given you everything you need to succeed. We have journeyed together to the base of the mountain and I have shared with you he tools needed to make the climb. It is now your time to make the assent to the summit."

We spent the yet few hours reviewing past joys and discussing future possibilities. Those hours were a mix of joy and sadness as good friends said their good-byes.

The next week I drove Fred to the airport and sent him on his way to New Mexico. Over the next few years, Fred and I stayed in touch and spent a week each year visiting. During those visits I met Fred's son William and daughter Elian. They both embodied the things Fred had taught me and we became friends very quickly.

It was a few years later on a Thursday morning when I got the call from Elian that Fred had passed away peacefully during the night. I attended the memorial service and as I suspected the church was filled with people.

I kept in touch with Fred's children and even consulted with them when I needed advice in their area of expertise.

EPILOGUE

I was reluctant to write this portion of the book, and it is only at the request of my brother that I do so. He says he has always been surprised at how well I deal with life's hardships and setbacks. He marvels at my ability to keep moving forward, never getting down or depressed, and always having a lust for life. He urged me to record how I am able to do this.

At first, I said, "I do not know what I do that is special; I just live life." Since then, I have given it a great deal of thought and have come up with a few answers. I will say that analyzing your own life is an enlightening experience. I will tell you a little about my life, and hopefully, you will see the disadvantages and distractions I have overcome. I have also noted the accomplishments afforded me by my approach to life. My life has not been as tough as many. But like you, it has seen calm seas and heavy storms. I offer you my life for your review.

My parents married when my dad was nineteen and my mom was fifteen. My mom was sixteen when I was born. She never finished high school. My dad graduated high school but went no further with formal education. Our family never had much money, and I would label us as lower-middle class. Despite that, or maybe because of it, we were a close-knit family. My family consisted of Mom, Dad, myself, two younger brothers, and one younger sister. Dad worked in a dairy running machinery, and was considered a skilled laborer. Mom stayed at home until the youngest of us was eleven. Then she took a part-time job at an ice cream store. Family finances lead me to a personal decision at about age fourteen. I was never going to be poor. In support of that resolution, I became the first member of my family to earn a college degree.

My parents could not afford to send me to college but offered what help they could. They said if I could pay for college, I could live at home rent-free while attending. I went one semester on money earned the previous summer. I studied electrical engineering and after that semester, I decided it was not for me. After my money ran out, I got my first full-time job. I still wanted a career in some type of engineering so I took a job making electrical cables for aircraft simulators. At the time, I figured that was as close to engineering as I could get. A year and a half later, I transferred to the company's drafting department as a trainee. After a few night school courses in drafting, my future career was set.

The pattern of part-time schooling was also set. I was in school every semester from age six through age fifty-three. All of my education was paid for from my earnings, a little at a time. I earned an associate degree at age twenty-seven, a bachelor's degree at age forty-eight, and a master's degree at age fifty-three. The master's is in human resource management and for a few years, I was on the editorial advisement committee of *Human Resource Magazine*. I started my career in engineering as a trainee draftsman and retired from Boeing Aircraft as a Senior Research Design Engineer.

During those years I contributed designs to both the Space shuttle and the Moon lander. I belonged to the American Society of Mechanical Engineers and the American Society of Optical Engineers. I hold two United States patents, with the second one also being awarded by England, France, and Germany. This is my second published book. I am blessed to have two wonderful sons and their families who are incredibly supportive. I am not what might be considered wealthy, but I believe myself successful. I am still at it; at age 82 I have opened my own travel agency.

My life has had setbacks, as will yours. Your emotional responses and how you handle them will have a great impact on your ability to achieve success.

During my life, I have had two unhappy divorces and one extremely happy marriage. The happy one was the last and ended after twenty-five years when my wife died of cancer. My first wife and I just drifted apart emotionally but had three wonderful children, two boys and a girl. My daughter, despite severe dyslexia, graduated college and went on to spend several years doing missionary work. It was on one of those trips that she contracted a rare disease that caused her blood to clot. The doctors were unable to identify the disease or stop the clotting. The illness finally took her at the age of twenty-six.

My second wife developed a grave mental illness causing several serious problems. She wrote many fraudulent checks. She called my children at all times of the day or night. During those calls, she would curse them and me or ramble on with disconnected thoughts. Once when I was working for Northrup Grumman Aircraft, she called the vice president of the company and demanded he make me return her calls. On one occasion, I came home to discover she had taken all my clothes and pictures of my children, thrown them into our back yard, and hosed them down. Most of the photos were damaged beyond saving. Those types of actions were constant over many months, and finally caused me to seek and obtain my second divorce.

My first two wives died relatively young and even though divorced, I was sorrowed by their passing. My third marriage was one of great joy, except at the very end.

During the last three months of her life, my third wife was in a battle she could not win. She was just fighting to give us more time together. I think during that time we were closer than ever and I am so grateful we had it.

Most of my approaches to a successful life have already been covered in the story of Fred Thomas. To satisfy my brother, I will review them here with one addition. It is my hope that the reader may find some usefulness herein.

Here is how I survived in my corner of the universe:

1. Be a nice person—help other people and they will help you. Be respectful and respect will be returned in kind.
2. Take responsibility—own your successes, failures, actions, and consequences.
3. Listen—listen to others and try to understand their point of view. Keep an open mind. It might be hard to believe, but someone else might have a better idea than yours.
4. When trying to solve a problem, focus on the solution, not on placing blame. If needed, addressing the "who caused the problem?" can be done following the solution. Remember, getting angry with someone is rarely the best resolution.
5. Understand there is nothing wrong with being successful or wealthy. The more successful you are, the better you can help others.
6. It is impossible to become successful without the help of others.
7. You were born with all you need to be successful.
8. You are an individual. There is no one like you, never has been, never will be. You deserve to be successful because you have things to offer that no one else has.
9. Success takes work, study, and preparation. Have a goal, and have a plan to achieve the goal.
10. Believe that you are successful and that you deserve success.

What do I believe contributes the most to my ability to overcome life's obstacles and move toward success? It is my absolute belief in myself. Do not misunderstand, no one becomes successful without lots of help from others, and I am no exception. It is belief in myself that allows me to take full advantage of that help. When making a decision, I seek advice and suggestions but the decision is mine, and I take responsibility for it. I am happy to take full credit for the good decision but just as quick to accept responsibility for a bad one. I do that knowing it was my decision and no one else's. I set my own goals, not those set for me by others. I am the one who decides what success is for me. Then I set my own goals and plans for reaching them.

During my working years, I put together a dynamic resume. Notice the action words "put together." It was not just a list of jobs I had held, skills I possessed, or other specific accomplishments designed to make the resume look good. It was deliberately constructed by me to reach the goal I had created for myself. For example, I knew I wanted to work in the engineering field. Before I became an engineer, I found someone to sponsor me so I could join The American Society of Mechanical Engineers, and that really looked good on the resume. The point is it did not happen by accident. I made it happen. Here is another example. Right after my second divorce, I felt like there was no marriage like I had envisioned.

As a result of divorce, I lost a lot financially and emotionally. I was not sure where my life was heading. That lasted about ten days. One day, I remember suddenly thinking, *You're better than this. You are stronger than this. Life is good and you deserve everything it has to offer.* That was the end of feeling down. I believed I deserved better and I was convinced I was in control of my future. I realized I still had me; this is really all any of us has. It is no on else's job to make you happy. It is your job to make yourself happy. As near as I can figure, this is how I get through life's tough times. Everyone is different so I do not claim this will work for you. I do claim that the ideas throughout this book will work for you or anyone.

If you have read this far and still feel you need someone's permission to succeed, you have missed the whole point of this book. You already possess the ability to be successful. The only person you need permission from is you. With permission from yourself, anything can happen; without it nothing will happen. It is like sitting in a car with the engine off and dreaming of taking a wonderful road trip. Until you start the car, it is all a dream of what could be. Giving yourself permission is your act of turning the key.

TEST—DO I DESERVE SUCCESS?

Benjamin Franklin was a smart guy, and he had an interesting way of reviewing a problem. It is an approach you might try to evaluate your worthiness for success.

Start with an eight and a half by eleven-inch piece of paper. Draw a line down the center and a line across an inch from the top. Label the top of the left column, "Why I Deserve Success." Label the right column, "Why I Do Not Deserve Success."

In the left column list all the reasons you think you deserve success. In the right column list the reasons you think you do not deserve success. This should give a good idea of your self-image.

Example of Test:

Why I Deserve Success:

I'm a nice person
I'm smart
I'm creative

Why I Do Not Deserve Success:

I do not have a college degree

MY RED BOOK ADDITIONS

THE TWO MOST RECENT ADDITIONS TO MY OWN LITTLE RED BOOK exemplify the expression, "It is not where you start, but where you finish that counts." I am sure the people in these next two examples are not finished with their accomplishments, but let's see where they are now compared to where they started.

The first is Barbara Corcoran. You might recognize her name if you watch the television show *Shark Tank*. On that show, wealthy business owners (the sharks) are introduced to entrepreneurs looking for someone to invest in their companies. Barbara Corcoran is one of the sharks. In 2015, she purchased a penthouse unit on New York City's 5th Avenue for an estimated 10 million dollars. She had successfully founded The Corcoran Group, a real estate brokerage firm. She later sold the firm for a reported 66 million dollars. She has written several books, appeared on NBC's *Today Show*, and hosted her own show on CNBC. Also, she is an in-demand speaker and business consultant.

So what was her beginning? She was from a family of ten children. Her mother was a homemaker, and her father had several jobs during her younger years. School was not easy for her because she suffered with dyslexia. Because of that, she graduated high school with below average grades. With determination, and despite the dyslexia, she went on to obtain a college degree in education.

After a year of teaching, she moved on to several different jobs including renting apartments, waitressing, and working as a receptionist. With a small loan from her friend, the two started their own company. Seven years later, the partnership ended, and Barbara went on to start her own company, The Corcoran Group. When you consider where she started and where she is today, it is an amazing story. I am not implying that if your life had a rough start you could become a millionaire. I am saying with hard work and determination, you can have a successful life.

The second recent addition to my little red book is Robert Herjavee. He is also a shark on the show *Shark Tank*. So why do I consider him an example of, "It's not where you start, but where you finish that counts?" Let's look at where he is today. He founded BRAK Systems, an integrator of security software. In 2000, he sold the company for $30.2 million. Just three years later, he formed Harjavee Group, a technology and computer security company. That company has an estimated annual revenue of $200 million. He graduated from New College at the University of Toronto with degrees in English literature and political science. He has written several books on business, been featured on CBC and ABC, and in 2012 was honored by the Canadian government for outstanding service to Canada. His estimated net worth is $200 million.

So where did he start? He was born in Varazdin, Croatia (former Yugoslavia). His family immigrated to Canada when Robert was eight. They arrived in Nova Scotia with one suitcase and twenty dollars. Robert found himself in strange surroundings and spoke no English. Approximately fourteen years later, he graduated from college with a degree in English literature. That is what I call determination and commitment. After working several different jobs, he applied for a job at Logiquest, selling IBM products. Knowing he lacked qualifications to work there, he offered to work for free for 6 months if given an opportunity. He was hired and worked his way up to general manger. After leaving Logiquest in 1990, he founded BRAK Systems in the basement of his home. He later sold it to AT&T Canada for $30.2 million.

These success stories are intended to answer those who say, "Don't expect too much from me, look where I came from." If you can read, you already own the one skill needed to acquire all the knowledge you will ever need. A good library can provide you with all the knowledge ever written.

If Robert Herjavee can become a millionaire with all the challenges he faced, think what you can accomplish knowing the culture, customs, and language of your own country.

Think about it. Then get started.

EXCERPTS FROM FRED'S LITTLE RED BOOK

THE FOLLOWING PAGES ARE EXCERPTS FROM FRED'S LITTLE RED BOOK.

PEOPLE

Example 1

He grew up in London in the 1820's. He got a little schooling before events changed the course of his future. His father lost the family's money, and was unable to pay his debts. He was sent to debtor's prison. Many of his father's family ended up in prison except for one son. The son avoided prison but at age twelve, he was put to work to help earn money. He worked on the assembly line of a shoe polish factory. He worked ten hour days for six shillings a week. He was able to return to school after his father paid off the debt. Once again though, school was cut short when he needed to work to help support his family. This time he worked as an office clerk. That eventually lead to becoming a reporter and writer. He received literary acclaim for his works such as *The Pickwick Papers, Oliver Twist,* and *David Copperfield*. Rather than be defeated by a tough beginning, Charles Dickens used those experiences to fascinate and entertain the world with his stories.

Example 2:

George was born in Baltimore, Maryland, and was one of eight children. His parents worked long hours, and had little time to provide George the guidance he needed. As a result, he started to miss school and get into trouble. His parents decided he needed more supervision than they could provide so at age seven they sent him to a boy's school run by the St. Xaverian Brothers. There he learned vocational skills and developed an interest in sports. He became so good at baseball that he came to the attention of Jack Dunn, owner of the Baltimore Orioles. Mr. Dunn was so impressed that he signed 19-year-old George to a contract. Because of his young age, George's team nicknamed him, "Jack's newest baby." He was optioned to the Red Sox, and later to the Yankees. The Yankee players shortened his nickname and added his real last name. He became the legend known as Babe Ruth. He ended up holding 56 major league records including a record for 714 home runs. Most people do not know that to reach those 714 home runs, Babe Ruth struck out 488 times. Clearly, he did not let his failures keep him from his successes. At his death, millions of people mourned his loss. Despite an unfortunate beginning, Babe Ruth had the drive to turn his gift into world recognition.

MYTHS ABOUT SUCCESS

Money is the root of all evil.

All work and no play make Johnny a dull boy.

Nice guys always finish last.

You need to be a workaholic to be successful.

An expensive education is required to be successful.

You should always look out for yourself before others.

You can network your way to the top.

Just expect success and it will come.

The successful person is the one with the most toys.

THOUGHTS ON SUCCESS

"To me, success is not outscoring someone, it is the peace of mind that comes from self-satisfaction in knowing you did your best. That's something each individual must determine." —John Wooden, college basketball coach

"Success is going from failure to failure without losing enthusiasm." —Winston Churchill, former Prime Minister of England

"Success does not consist in never making a misstate, but in never making the same one a second time." —George Bernard Shaw, playwright

"When I've been unsuccessful, I've been controlled. When I've been successful, I've been in control." —Katherine Hepburn, actor

"Success to me is being a good person, treating people well." —David Lachapelle, artist

"A successful man is one who can lay a firm foundation with the bricks others have thrown at him." —David Brinkly, news commentator

"Get around people who talk about vision and ideas, not other people." —Author unknown

NUMBERS

"Entrepreneurs average 3.8 failures before final success...."
—Lisa M Amos, business information provider

There are 1,700 new millionaires per day in the United States.

Ninety-five percent of choices are based on emotion and feeling; only 5% are based on logic and reason.

Only 20% of people set life goals for themselves and of that number, only 30% work toward and reach them.

The English language contains approximately 250,000 words and three times that many meanings for those words.

Thirty percent of the world's billionaires do not have college degrees.

Only 10% more effort than others will put you in the group considered "high performers."

Seventy-six is the life expectancy of the average American male.

If you are paid weekly, after starting work at age 21, and retire at age 65, you will only receive 2,288 weekly pay checks in your lifetime.

DEFINITIONS

Attitude—a settled way of thinking or feeling about someone or something, typically one that is reflected in a person's behavior. Individuality and self-confidence as manifested by behavior.

Commitment—a state or quality of being dedicated to a cause or activity. A pledge or understanding.

Focus—a central point, as of attraction, attention, or activity.

Goal—the result or achievement toward which effort is directed.

Perseverance—a continued effort to do or achieve something despite difficulties, failure, or opposition.

Persistence—existing for a long or longer than usual time, or continuously: such as retained beyond the usual period.

Option—the power or right of choosing.

Success—the favorable or prosperous termination of attempts or endeavors, the accomplishment of a goal.

MY THANKS

You have my thanks for taking time to consider my thoughts. It is my sincere hope that you gained something of value from your read. Congratulations on now owning your own little red book.

ABOUT THE AUTHOR

Forney Shell holds a Bachelor's degree in Business Management and a Master's degree in Human Resource Management. Forney retired for Boeing Aircraft with the title of Senior Research Design Engineer and contributed his designs to the Space Shuttle and Moon lander. He is the owner of Pan Piper Travel and a former professor at the college of business and Technology in Charlottesville, Virginia.

www.ingramcontent.com/pod-product-compliance
Lightning Source LLC
Chambersburg PA
CBHW071913070526
44583CB00016B/1970